MEN-AT-ARMS SERIES

EDITOR: MARTIN WINDRO

ALBAN BOOK SERVICES

Napoleon's Polish Troops

Text by OTTO VON PIVKA

Colour plates by MICHAEL ROFFE

OSPREY PUBLISHING LIMITED

Published in 1974 by
Osprey Publishing Ltd, P.O. Box 25,
707 Oxford Road, Reading, Berkshire
© Copyright 1974 Osprey Publishing Ltd

cased edition ISBN 0 85045 227 9
paper edition ISBN 0 85045 198 1

Printed in Great Britain by
Jarrold & Sons Ltd, Norwich

Introduction

On 25 November 1795 the kingdom of Poland fell prey to her stronger neighbours, Russia, Prussia and Austria, and the third partition of that unhappy, turbulent state took place.

The elected King of Poland, Stanislas Augustus, was forced to abdicate and retired to Russia with a pension of 200,000 ducats a year. He died at St Petersburg (now Leningrad) on 12 February 1798.

His old kingdom was redistributed as follows:

Austria took the larger part of the palatinate of Krakow, the palatinates of Sandomir and Lublin and part of the district of Chelm and those parts of the palatinates of Brzecz, Podlachie and Mazovie which lay on the left bank of the River Bug.

Prussia took those parts of Podlachie and Mazovie which lay on the right bank of the Bug; part of the palatinates of Troki and Samogitie situated on the left bank of the Niemen and one district of the palatinate of Krakow.

Russia took the rest of Lithuania up to the River Niemen, the rest of the palatinates of Brzecz and Novogrodek and the greater part of Samogitie and the remains of Wolhynie, Courland and Semigalle.

France alone had opposed Poland's treatment and became the natural refuge of all Polish exiles. Many Polish officers and men were still held as prisoners of war in Tobolsk, Petersburg, Moscow, Olmütz, Magdeburg and other places, but among those in Paris was one General Jean-Henri Dombrowski who on 11 October 1796 formed the 'Polish Legion' with Napoleon's aid.

As Article 287 of the French Constitution did not permit the presence of foreign troops on French soil, Dombrowski was sent to Italy to complete his work in the new republic created as a result of Napoleon's victories in Italy. After the victory of Lodi, the Cispadane and Transpadane Republics were combined into the Cisalpine Republic, and the government of this new state, being unable to raise its own army, decided to enlist the aid of foreign troops.

Dombrowski arrived in Milan on 2 December 1796 and presented his scheme to Napoleon. On 4 January 1797 Napoleon wrote to the Council of State of Lombardy to say that General Dombrowski was willing to raise a Polish legion to help the people of Lombardy. Napoleon added that he would gladly take all measures necessary for this operation.

This offer was well received and on 9 January 1797 a convention was signed by which Dombrowski guaranteed the services of his compatriots to the republic in exchange for which his men became Lombard citizens and received the same pay and privileges as the other national troops. The Poles retained their own uniforms and commands were given in Polish. They wore the French cockade and contre-epaulettes in Lombardy's national colours with the inscription 'Gli uomini liberi sono fratelli' (Free men are brothers).

Napoleon at the tomb of Frederick the Great, Potsdam.

Crests of the joint kingdom of Poland-Lithuania (left) and Saxony (right) on a Saxon cannon cast in 1707 and now in Coburg Castle.

On 20 January 1797 Dombrowski published a proclamation in four languages calling on Poles to enter his new legion.

Two weeks later the Legion consisted of 1,200 men in Polish uniform (kurtka, pantaloons and czapka in blue cloth).

Many of his men came from the Austrian Army which included in its ranks officers and soldiers originally from Galicia and many others were Polish ex-prisoners of war and deserters.

In March the Legion was sent to the fortress of Mantua, where it was joined by a new battalion. At the same time its artillery was organized at Milan. It did not receive its baptism of fire until the insurrection at Brescia.

By April, Dombrowski had 5,000 men enrolled.

Dombrowski, anxious for action, wanted his legion augmented by 2,000 infantry, 500 cavalry and sixty cannon from the Army of Italy in order to undertake a raid through Croatia, Transylvania and Hungary up into Galicia. This was almost approved, and on 18 April the Legion was at the Leoben Pass preparing to march when Napoleon forbade the scheme on the grounds that it would not serve the political good of the Polish cause.

At this time occurred the massacre at Verona and the troubles in Venice; the Legion took an active part in the assault on Verona.

In May the Legion had so increased in size that it was reorganized into two infantry legions, the first commanded by General Kniaziewicz, the second by General Wielhorski.

Each consisted of three battalions of ten companies, each company having 125 men. The corps also had three companies of artillery commanded by Chef de bataillon Axamitowski.

French regulations were used for garrison duties; drill and discipline were according to old Polish regulations but corporal punishment was forbidden, as was the case in the French Army of the day.

In July 1797 Dombrowski and the grenadier battalion went to suppress the insurrection at Reggio during which the Poles much distinguished themselves.

At the end of 1798 the Neapolitan Army invaded the Papal state to expel the Franco-Polish forces under General Championnet. Kniaziewicz commanded the Polish Legion during Dombrowski's absence and on 4 December the Neapolitans were defeated at the Battle of Civita Castellana. From the captured stocks of horses and harness found in Gaete arsenal after this battle, a regiment of cavalry was added to the Polish Legion.

The new regiment was commanded by Colonel Karwowski; Elie Tremo and Biernacki were nominated Chefs d'Escadrons. Organization was not complete, however, before the armistice of 11 January. On 23 January Naples capitulated and as a mark of respect to the Polish services, General Kniaziewicz was sent to Paris by General Championnet to take back all the trophies captured during the campaign.

A new anti-French coalition was quickly formed and considerable Austro-Russian forces under the command of the Russian Feld Marschall Leutnant

Eagle of the 13th Infantry and (right) both sides of the flag of the 1st Battalion, 14th Infantry.

Suvarow soon advanced to threaten the young republics founded in Italy.

Forces available for their defence were few. The élite French troops were in Egypt with Napoleon; the command of the Army of Italy was held by the incompetent Scherer; Championnet had gone and was replaced as commander of the army of Naples by Macdonald.

The Polish Legions, commanded by Wielhorski and Rynkiewicz, were garrisoned in Mantua at the start of the campaign and were employed dispersed amongst the French units. Constantly engaged in different battles, they suffered heavily; from 26 March to 5 April (after the Battle of Magnano where General Rynkiewicz was killed). Of the 4,000 men who had set out, only 2,000 effectives remained. The Second Legion retired into Mantua with their artillery under the command of Wielhorski. Mantua was commanded by General Foissac-Latour and was besieged and capitulated (much against the wishes of the Polish officers) on 28 July. The Austrians demanded the return to their service of all Poles coming from

Napoleon Bonaparte. Engraving after a drawing made from life in Milan.

Scene from the Revolutionary wars in northern Italy; Austrian infantry about to attack the French.

Austrian-controlled Galicia and all had to revert to the rank of private regardless of what position they had attained in the Legion. Axamitowski and 150 men of the Legion escaped to Lyons disguised in French uniforms. General Wielhorski, Major Kosinski and the officers were imprisoned in Leoben and did not regain their freedom until after the Battle of Marengo.

This was the end of the Second Legion.

The First Legion, augmented by the battalions of grenadiers and voltigeurs of Malachowski and Jasinski and by Karwowski's cavalry regiment were directly·under Dombrowski's command.

Together with two French demi-brigades they were responsible for establishing communications between the Army of Italy and the Army of Naples.

After May the First Legion and a French demi-brigade formed the 1st Division of the joint army. There followed the Battle of Trebbia (17, 18 and 19 June) after which the French army withdrew to Genoa, the Battle of Novi (15 August) and the Battle of Zürich (26 September) which finally broke the forces of the Austro-Russian coalition.

Following the disasters which dogged the French in Italy the Cisalpine Republic disappeared and the homeless debris of the Legion found themselves in France where they promptly set about raising a new legion.

Conditions in France had changed; Bonaparte left Egypt secretly and landed at Frejus on 2 October 1799. On 9 November he changed the form of French government and was proclaimed First Consul. He decreed that foreign troops could be taken into French service and ordered the formation of new legions.

On 10 February 1800 the remnants of the Polish-Italian Legions were reorganized at Marseilles and renamed 'La Légion Italique'. Kniaziewicz meanwhile had received orders to form another Polish legion; this formation, the 'Legion of the Danube', was organized as follows:

Four battalions of infantry each of ten companies of 123 men
One regiment of cavalry of four squadrons
One battery of horse artillery

Its strength was 5,970 men and the commanders were:

Legion commander	General Kniaziewicz
Chief of Staff	Gawrowski
Chef de Brigade	Sokolnicki
Chefs de bataillons	Fiszer, Drzewiecki, Kralewski and Wasilewski
Artillery battery	Redel

In March 1800 the infantry of the Danube Legion went to the Rhine and joined the corps of General St Suzanne on the left wing of the 'Armée du Rhin'. They fought at the actions of Berg, Bernheim and Offenburg and occupied the fortress of Philipsbourg after the armistice of Parsdorf (15 July 1800).

The Danube Legion was also engaged at the Battle of Hohenlinden on 3 December 1800. A lancer of the Legion, Jan Pawlikowski, disarmed and captured fifty-seven Austrians single-handed. Completely illiterate, he refused General Moreau's offer of a commission and a financial reward and was content with the rank of sergeant and the presentation of a carbine of honour from the French Government bearing the inscription: 'La Republique française à son defenseur, le citoyen

6

Marshal Masséna, Duc de Rivoli, Prince d'Essling; his invasion of Portugal in 1810 was halted by the Lines of Torres Vedras.

artillery company. After serving at the sieges of Peschiera and Mantua, they returned to Milan.

The Peace of Luneville (26 January 1801) ended the war but did not bring about the liberation of Poland. In protest, Kniaziewicz resigned his command of the Danube Legion and General Jablonowski took his place.

Dombrowski retained command of the (Polish) Italian Legion and both this formation and the Legion of the Danube were reviewed by him at Milan on 21 March 1801. At this time the Italian Legion had 303 officers and 6,432 men; the Danube Legion had about 6,000 all ranks.

The temporary peaceful climate in Europe did nothing to aid the Polish cause; on 21 December 1801 the French Government disbanded both Polish Legions and converted them into three foreign 'demi-brigades' (a new term coined by General Carnot, French Army reformer).

The Italian Legion (the old 1st Polish Legion) became the '1er and 2e Demi-Brigade Étrangère', the old Danube Legion became the '3e Demi-Brigade Étrangère'. By 18 May 1802 this latter formation, now renumbered the '113e Demi-Brigade' and consisting of 118 officers and 2,235

Jan Pawlikowski, lancier de la cavalerie polonaise, qui pendant le bataille de 12 frimaire de l'an IX de la Republique, fit 57 prisonniers.'

The campaign ended on 25 December 1800.

Dombrowski, meanwhile, was organizing the 'Italian Legion' in Marseilles after the 1799 campaign. Consisting of 9,000 men, the Legion had seven infantry battalions and five companies of artillery.

The Polish troops now released from the fortress of Mantua formed the cadres of the 4th, 5th and 6th battalions of the Legion; the cadre for the 7th Battalion came from the 1st, 2nd and 3rd battalions of the Legion.

Karwowski's cavalry regiment was sent to join the Danube Legion. The remainder of the new recruits for both legions came from men of Polish origin among the Austrian prisoners of war now held in France.

On 8 November 1800 the Italian Legion under Dombrowski joined the Army of Italy (commanded now by Masséna, who had replaced Championnet). Their strength at this point was 5,000 men in four infantry battalions and one

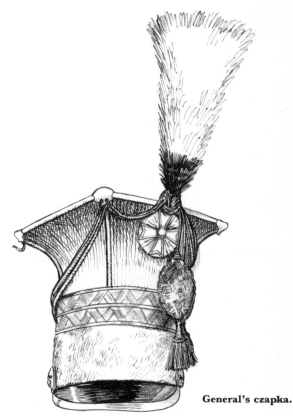

General's czapka.

7

men in three battalions commanded by Zagarski, Bolesta and Pierre Wierbycki, was forcibly embarked at Livorno for service in the French West Indian colony of Saint Domingue. Two French demi-brigades had 'escorted' the Poles on to the transports.

The 2e Demi-Brigade Étrangère suffered a like fate; renumbered the 114e Demi-Brigade, they were 'escorted' on to transports in Genoa with a strength of eighty-seven officers and 2,750 men and set sail, also for Saint Domingue, at the beginning of February 1803.

Of these two demi-brigades only about fifteen officers and 150 men returned to Europe; the rest had been killed in action or had died of yellow fever or were now in the English prison hulks.

The 1er Demi-Brigade Étrangère was incorporated into the 1st Italian Division of the army of the newly formed Cisalpine Republic. They were present at the blockade of Venice under General St Cyr and fought the Austrians under the Duc de Rohan at the Battle of Castel-Franco. In 1806 they entered Naples with the corps of General St Cyr to secure that state for its new king, Joseph, Napoleon's younger brother. They were still there when the Prussians were crushed at Jena and Auerstadt by Napoleon on 14 October 1806. Dombrowski was called to Paris to discuss with the Emperor his plans for the reorganization of Poland.

The Grand Duchy of Warsaw

Having effectively destroyed the Prussian Army at Jena, and forced Saxony and the Saxon duchies to abandon Prussia and to become his allies, Napoleon proceeded to defeat Russia and the remnants of the Prussian Army at the battles of Preussisch Eylau (7 and 8 February 1807) and Friedland (14 June 1807).

The culmination of the campaign was the Treaty of Tilsit, signed between Napoleon, Tsar

Napoleon reviews his Guard in the Lustgarten, Berlin, after smashing the Saxon-Prussian Army at Jena and Auerstadt.

Alexander I of Russia and King Friedrich Wilhelm III of Prussia on a raft moored in the centre of the River Niemen. One of the results of this treaty was the creation of the 'Grand Duchy of Warsaw' under nominal control of the King of Saxony who had been promoted from his previous rank of Kurfürst (Prince-elector of the Holy Roman Empire) by Napoleon for his support in the recent campaign.

The creation of the grand duchy was far below the aim set by Dombrowski and his compatriots Joseph Wybicki and Kosciuszko who had pressed Napoleon to reconstitute the independent Polish state in her borders of 1795.

In exchange for a dubiously worded promise from Napoleon to give the Poles back their homeland, a guard of honour of about one hundred riders was formed in Posen in November 1806 and command of this unit was given to Uminski who had been aide-de-camp to the Polish General Madalinski in the 1795 campaign.

Napoleon's progress through the old Polish areas was a series of delirious triumphs and the Posen 'Garde d'honneur' replaced the Emperor's own French troops.

The French advanced guard of Davout's corps entered Warsaw on 28 November, and Napoleon followed on 17 December.

The 'Polish honeymoon' was soon over; the retreating Prussians and Russians had destroyed those stores which they could not carry away, but Napoleon insisted that the country provide his rapacious army with supplies or he would hand Poland back to her previous oppressors.

The Poles had to find 100,000 rations of food per day for their French liberators and a reserve of 300,000 rations was to be held in the depots. The conduct of the French troops in the duchy soon led to a drastic cooling of Franco-Polish relations.

Dombrowski now set about recruiting men for the new forces of the duchy and this scheme was heartily supported by Napoleon.

A wealth of irregular units existed and Dombrowski formalized these into, initially, four infantry and two cavalry regiments. All officers down to the rank of captain had seen service under the old Polish eagle, only the junior officers were new to military life.

By 30 December 1806 Dombrowski had 30,000 men including 600 cavalry concentrated at Posen. In January 1807 Napoleon directed that the 1st Battalions of the eight newly formed Polish line infantry regiments were to go to Bromberg to join the Grande Armée. Each battalion was 800 men strong, and Dombrowski commanded the division which was divided into two brigades, the 1st (under General Axamitowski) consisting of the 1st–4th Infantry Regiments and the 1st Chasseurs à Cheval; the 2nd Brigade (General Fiszer) included the 5th–8th Infantry Regiments and the 2nd Chasseurs à Cheval. Total divisional strength was 6,400 men including 300 cavalry. There was also one battery of foot artillery of six guns.

A regiment of 'National Cavalry' of three squadrons each of 120 men and the 'Levée Noble' (three regiments of volunteers) also came to Bromberg later to strengthen Dombrowski's cavalry.

At the same time, the old 'Italian Legion' (General Grabinski's demi-brigade) also joined the army with three battalions of infantry each 800 strong, and Colonel Rozniecki's regiment of lancers.

Another newly raised Polish force was the 'Légion du Nord' of 2,500 men under Prince Michel Radziwill; this legion had been raised on the Rhine from Austrian and Prussian prisoners

The city of Warsaw in about 1760, by Bellotto.

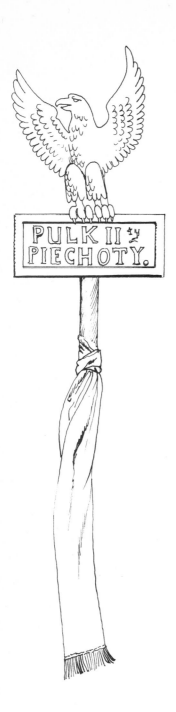

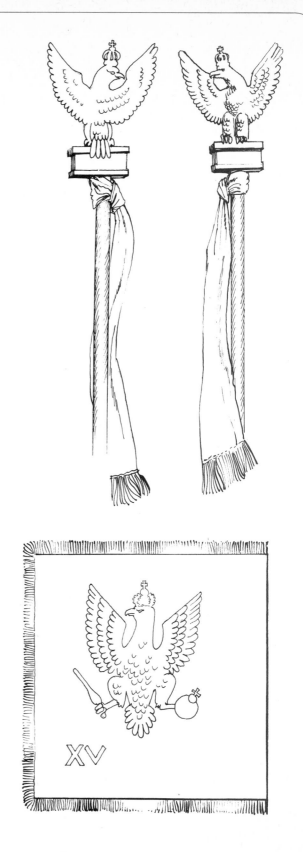

(Right) The crimson and silver standard of the
15th Polish Lancers; (Above left) the eagle of the
11th Polish Infantry Regiment; (Above right)
front and back views of Polish eagles.

of Polish extraction. It was sent to join the Siege of Danzig.

By a decree of 14 January 1807 Napoleon empowered the Polish Government to negotiate peace settlements with Prussia and Russia and on 23 January Dombrowski's division was sent to join Marshal Lefebvre's X Corps at the Siege of Danzig. General Zajonczek, with four newly raised Polish battalions (formed at Kalisz), joined the French forces besieging Graudenz and some days later Napoleon gave Prince Poniatowski command of six other newly formed Polish battalions for garrison duty in Warsaw. The Posen 'Garde d'honneur' was now attached to the Imperial Guard as the '1st Regiment of Polish Chevau-Légers'.

While the main French Army was beating the Russians at Preussisch Eylau on 8 February 1807, the V and X Corps were employed reducing those Prussian fortresses which still held out in his rear.

In front of Danzig, Dombrowski captured Dirschau on 23 February 1807, capturing seven

Prince Josef Poniatowski, after a contemporary engraving in Dresden. Note the traditional Polish headgear – czapka– the general's lace at the collar (still worn today on the shoulder-straps of Polish generals) and the elaborate tasselled harness.

cannon and 800 men. Napoleon distributed fourteen crosses of the Legion of Honour among the Poles for this action.

The forces besieging Danzig consisted of Dombrowski's division (6,000 men), the Legion du Nord (2,500 men), a division from Baden, and 3,000 French troops.

Danzig capitulated on 26 May 1807 and subsequently became an independent republic. Four thousand Poles from the Danzig garrison joined Dombrowski's force.

The Polish Chevau-légers Regiment attached to the Imperial Guard was incorporated into this élite body of the French Army by an imperial decree of 6 April 1807 issued from Napoleon's headquarters at Finkenstein as the 'Regiment de chevaulégers polonaise de la garde'.

On 14 June 1807 Napoleon defeated Russia at the Battle of Friedland and Dombrowski's division (part of Mortier's corps) earned French praise for their conduct in this action. Polish losses were eleven officers and 525 men dead and wounded.

Standard of the 1st *Chasseurs à cheval*: silver eagle and base, gold crown and lettering on dark blue ground; crimson cloth, silver fringes, cords, tassels, eagle and script.

11

Each infantry regiment had three battalions each of six companies including one grenadier, one voltigeur and four fusilier companies (the standard French Army system).

THE INFANTRY REGIMENT

Staff of a regiment of infantry:
One Colonel
One Major
Three Chefs de bataillon
One Paymaster
Three Adjutant-majors
One Colour bearer (*Port-aigle*)
One Surgeon 1st Class
Two Surgeons 2nd Class
Three Surgeons 3rd Class
One Chaplain
Six Adjutants N.C.O.s
Two N.C.O.s (2nd and 3rd
    Porte-aigle)
One Regimental drum major
One Battalion drum major
Eight Musicians
Three Master Craftsmen
    (armourer, tailor and
    bootmaker)

Officers of the three battalions:
Six Captains 1st Class
Six Captains 2nd Class
Six Captains 3rd Class
Nine Lieutenants 1st Class
Nine Lieutenants 2nd Class
Eighteen Second Lieutenants

Each company consisted of:
One Captain
One Lieutenant
One Second Lieutenant
One Sergeant-major [*sic*]
Four Sergeants [*sic*]
One Fourrier (company
    quartermaster)
Eight Corporals
Two Drummers
117 Soldiers

THE CAVALRY REGIMENT

Each cavalry regiment has four squadrons each of two companies except the Kürassier regiment which only had two squadrons.

Regimental staff:
One Colonel
One Major
Two Chefs d'escadrons
One Paymaster
Two Adjutant-majors
One Surgeon 1st Class
Two Surgeons 2nd Class
Two Surgeons 3rd Class
One Chaplain
One Standard bearer
Two Adjutant N.C.O.s
One Trumpet major
One Veterinarian
Five Master Craftsmen
    (armourer, tailor, boot-
    maker, breeches-maker and
    saddler)

Regimental officers:
Three Captains 1st Class
Five Captains 2nd Class
Four Lieutenants 1st Class
Four Lieutenants 2nd Class
Sixteen Second Lieutenants

Each company consisted of:
One Captain
One Lieutenant
Two Second Lieutenants
One Maréchal des logis chef
    (sergeant-major)
Four Sergeants [sic]
One Fourrier
Eight Corporals
One Farrier (blacksmith)
Two Trumpeters
79 Troopers

One of the companies was the 'élite company'.

The Kürassier regiment of two squadrons had the following regimental staff:
One Colonel
One Major
One Chef d'escadron
One Paymaster
One Surgeon 1st Class
One Surgeon 2nd Class
Two Surgeons 3rd Class
One Chaplain
One Porte-etendard
One Trumpet major
One Veterinary surgeon
Five Master Craftsmen
    (as for the other regiments)

Each company had the same establishment as the other cavalry companies.

ARMY ORGANIZATION

GENERAL STAFF

Commander-in-Chief	Prince Joseph Poniatowski Général de Division
Chief of Staff	Général de Brigade Kamienecki
Comm. of the Artillery	Général de Brigade Axamitowski
Insp.-Gen. of Infantry	Général de Brigade Fiszer
Insp.-Gen. of Cavalry	Général de Brigade Rozniecki

1ST DIVISION

Commander: Général de Division	Prince Joseph Poniatowski
Chief of Staff: Major de Division	Colonel J. Paszkowski

INFANTRY BRIGADE

Général de Brigade	Luc Bieganski
1st Regiment	Colonel Micjel Grabowski
2nd Regiment	Colonel Comte Stanislaus Potocki

3rd Regiment	Colonel Zoltowski
4th Regiment	Colonel Comte Felix Potocki

CAVALRY BRIGADE

Commander: Général de Brigade	Stanislas Wojczynski
1st Regiment of Chasseurs	Colonel Michel Dombrowski, later Przebendowski
2nd Regiment of Lancers	Colonel Comte Thadee Tyszkiewicz

FOOT ARTILLERY

1st Battalion   Chef de Bataillon J. Redel

AN ENGINEER DETACHMENT

2nd DIVISION

Général de Division	Zajonczek
Chef d'Etat Major	Colonel Kossecki
Major de Division	Skorzewski (Paul)

INFANTRY

Général de Brigade	Comte Isidore Krasinski
5th Regiment*	Colonel Prince Michel Radziwill
6th Regiment	Colonel Valentin Skorzewski
7th Regiment	Colonel Sobolewski
8th Regiment	Colonel Godebski

CAVALRY

Général de Brigade	Niemojewski
3rd Regiment of Lancers	Colonel Lonczynski
4th Regiment of Chasseurs	Colonel Kwasniewski

FOOT ARTILLERY

2nd Battalion   Chef de Bataillon Gorski

AN ENGINEER DETACHMENT

3RD DIVISION

Commander: Général de Division	Jean Henri Dombrowski
Chief of Staff: Major de Division	Colonel Cz Pakosz

INFANTRY BRIGADE

Commander: Général de Brigade	Amilcar Kosinski
9th Regiment	Colonel Prince Antoine Sulkowski

10th Regiment	Colonel Downarowicz
11th Regiment	Colonel Mielzynski
12th Regiment	Colonel Poninski

CAVALRY BRIGADE

Commander: General de Brigade	M. Sokolnicki
5th Regiment of Chasseurs	Colonel Turno
6th Regiment of Lancers	Colonel Dom Dziewanowski

FOOT ARTILLERY

3rd Battalion   Chef de Bataillon Hurtig

AN ENGINEER DETACHMENT

In 1807 the army of the Grand Duchy of Warsaw comprised 31,713 infantry, 6,035 cavalry and 95 guns including the horse artillery battery formed at private expense by the young Count Wladimir Potocki.

Three French officers were attached to help organize the artillery and the engineers.

At the same time the regiment of Chevau-légers of the Guard was organized in the camp at Mir. Its colonel was the Count Vincent Krasinski and the four squadron commanders were Thomas Lubienski, Jan Kozietulski, Ignace Stolowski and Henri Kamienski.

The old 'Polish-Italian Legion' arrived in Silesia with General Grabinski and remained in the kingdom of Westfalia in order to reorganize. Comprising 6,000 men, it received the name of the 'Legion of the Vistula' and was divided into three regiments each of two battalions:

1st Regiment	Colonel Chlopicki Major Konsinowski Chefs de Bataillon – Ruthie and Fondzielski
2nd Regiment	Colonel Bialowiejski Major Szott
3rd Regiment	Colonel Swiderski Major Billing

* The 5th Regiment was the old Légion du Nord which had distinguished itself at the Siege of Danzig. Attached to Milhaud's division it had remained as garrison of that place in the pay of France. At the time of the creation of the Grand Duchy of Warsaw it was given the choice of remaining in French service or joining the forces of the new duchy. On 11 August the men were reviewed and the question posed: each company roared 'Niech z y je Polksa!' (Long live Poland!)

Those French officers in the Legion demanded to be retained in French service. The Legion became the 5th Infantry Regiment of the duchy and arrived in Warsaw at the beginning of May 1808.

The cavalry of the Legion (Lancers of the Vistula), who later became the 7th Lancers of the French Army, received Colonel Klicki as commander in place of Colonel Rozniecki who became Inspector-General of the Cavalry.

At the beginning of November General Grabinski received the order to reorganize his units prior

Fusilier's czapka, 7th Polish Infantry Regiment.

The hat of a Polish soldier of 1973, showing clearly the eagle badge, still exactly as it was in 1807 except for the removal of the crown.

to being incorporated into the French Army. All officers and men chose to serve their own country, but Napoleon was adamant and the Legion was sent to Kassel in the service of the newly formed kingdom of Westfalia.

Marshal Davout, who had French and foreign troops under his command, was in reality the military viceroy of the Grand Duchy of Warsaw with supreme control over the civil authorities.

On 1 September 1807 the Graf von Schönfeld, Minister Plenipotentiary of the King of Saxony, arrived in Warsaw; on 5 September he assembled the Provisional Government, dissolved it and created by royal decree in its place a government of one ministry having six members, almost all the members of the old regime.

Stanislas Malachowski was President of the Council, Prince Poniatowski retained the folio of War Minister.

On 21 September 1807 the King of Saxony, Duke of Warsaw, was received at the frontier by the President of the Council, the ministers and by General Dombrowski and arrived in state in the capital with his wife and daughter. Frederick Augustus liked the Poles and spoke their language well; he was good, just and pious but was no soldier.

The Saxon king remained in Warsaw until 21 December 1807, and on his departure he reinstated the order 'Virtuti Militari' which had been created by Stanislas-Augustus, and decorated many officers into its various grades. He introduced a modification: the horsed warrior on the reverse of the cross (the same as on the arms of Lithuania) was superseded by the motto 'Rex et patria'.

He wanted thus to avoid offending the Tsar of Russia (Alexander I) under whose control Lithuania now was.

After the king's departure the duchy continued its reorganization; in April 1808 it was divided into 'departments' on the French model.

In view of the reduction of the financial burden of the Polish Army which had been a drain on the Imperial Chest, Napoleon was able to pay from his own account a third of the sum which was required for the raising and equipping of the Poles.

He also ordered Marshal Davout to pay at the

The Battle of Aspern, 1809: the Austrian regiment Benjowski assaults the French in the burning church of Aspern.

end of June all that was required for the maintenance of the French Corps within the duchy whose expenses were originally to have been met by the Polish Treasury.

This made a good impression on all as the Polish Treasury was not in any condition to meet all these charges.

Not until the beginning of September 1808 did the French troops retire into Silesia, with Breslau as their headquarters.

The Marshal retained supreme command over the Polish Army but conferred direct control of the three Polish divisions on Prince Poniatowski. He continued to exercise political surveillance over the duchy and appointed one of his own officers, Colonel Saulnier, to be Commandant of Warsaw.

The Poles in Spain

At the outset of the Spanish campaign in spring 1808 the Polish contribution numbered some 8,000 men of the Vistula Legion and the Chevau-légers of the Guard, raised to 16,000 in August by the arrival of the 4th, 7th and 9th Infantry Regiments. The Vistula Legion infantry distinguished themselves at the two sieges of Saragossa; by the final fall of the city on 20 February 1809 the Legion had lost 1,390 men – thirty per cent casualties. The lancers of the Legion fought at Medina del Rio Seco. For the re-invasion of Spain in Novem-

Comte de Lasalle, one of Napoleon's generals.

The most famous action of the Vistula lancers in Spain was their devastating charge at Albuera on 16 May 1811, when, with a French hussar regiment, they annihilated Colborne's British infantry brigade.

The Chevau-légers of the Guard entered Spain with Napoleon, with a strength of eight companies. They distinguished themselves in a bloody charge at Somosierra on 30 November 1808, and took part in the pursuit of Moore's British Army to Astorga. After escorting the Emperor back to France they were stationed on the Franco-Spanish frontier, returning to Paris in February 1809. In February 1810, newly armed with lances and redesignated *Chevau-légers lanciers*, a detachment returned to northern Spain. They operated mainly against guerrilla bands in the area; present at Fuentes de Oñoro in May 1811, they did not in fact charge. In September 1811, 315 strong, this detachment returned to the parent regiment in France.

In February 1812 all Polish units serving in Spain were concentrated on the Ebro. Together the four regiments of the Vistula Legion had 3,000 men; the four infantry regiments of the duchy – the 4th, 7th and 9th – totalled 2,400; and the 7th, 8th and 9th Lancers totalled 1,000. (These figures were only achieved after reinforcement drafts from Warsaw.) Estimates of Polish casualties in this bitter campaign run as high as 40,000 dead and wounded; they consistently fought with great determination, and often, it must be said, displayed bestial cruelty.

ber 1808 the Legion served with Moncey's III Corps, and the other three infantry regiments with Lefebvre's IV Corps. The IV Corps regiments fought at Talavera on 28 July 1809, and at Almonacid on 10 August: they were prominent in the victory at Ocaña on 19 November 1809. Meanwhile the Legion had been employed in the eastern provinces, under Suchet. In March 1810 a fourth regiment joined the Legion infantry; it had originally been raised as a '2nd Legion of the Vistula' by a decree of 8 July 1809. The last battle in which the Legion took part in Spain was at Sagunto on 25 October 1811, where they provided the backbone of a French force of 18,000 which smashed 30,000 Spaniards.

The Vistula Legion lancers served separately from the infantry. A second regiment was raised by decree on 7 February 1811, under Colonel Lubienski, late of the Chevau-légers of the Guard; but on 18 June 1811 both regiments were incorporated into the French Army as the 7th and 8th Regiments of Lancers, a 9th regiment being formed around drafts from the other two. Only Poles were admitted to these three regiments.

In Poland, 1809

In the spring of 1809 Austria declared war on France, encouraged by signs of patriotic unrest among France's German vassals. At this stage the army of the Duchy of Warsaw consisted of the following: twelve infantry regiments each of three battalions; six cavalry regiments (1st, 4th and 5th Chasseurs à Cheval, 2nd, 3rd and 6th Lancers); three battalions of artillery, each of three companies, total ninety-three cannon; three engineer and three train companies. The 4th, 7th and 9th Infantry had been detached for Spanish service, and the 8th, 10th and 11th were in Modlin and Danzig. This left 11,265 infantry, 4,584 cavalry and 1,548 artillery for the defence of the duchy. Three divisions were formed, each of four infantry and two cavalry regiments and an artillery battalion, with the 1st Division also having a horse artillery battery. Some 2,200 Saxon troops were also available. This army was threatened by the Austrian VII Corps in Galicia, some 33,000 men under the Archduke Ferdinand.

Ferdinand invaded the duchy on 15 April 1809,

Major von Schill, the Prussian hussar officer who sparked off the north German campaign of 1809 when he took his regiment on a rampage through French-controlled territory. He was killed at Stralsund during the campaign.

and the first serious clash took place at Raszyn, some ten miles south-east of Warsaw, on 20 April. Poniatowski withdrew into Warsaw that night, and at this point the Saxon troops were recalled; the Poles had only 9,500 effectives left, and had to abandon Warsaw and retire into Modlin. A treaty was concluded making Warsaw a neutral city, and Poniatowski gathered strength. Austrian attempts to capture the Polish bridgehead which remained on their side of the Vistula at Praga were repulsed, and a successful counter-attack was mounted. Ferdinand next attacked Thorn, but withdrew when the Poles promptly threatened his rear in Galicia by taking Sandomir. Many of the 4,000 Austrians ejected were new local recruits, and some 800 immediately came over to the Poles. On 19/20 May Zamosc fell to the Poles; and the 3rd, 6th and 12th Polish infantry, with cavalry and artillery support, successfully resisted an attempt by 8,000 Austrians under Schauroth to recapture Sandomir. In the face of these repeated set-backs, and growing local resistance, Ferdinand abandoned Warsaw on 2 June 1809.

The situation became more complicated when

General Junot, Duc d'Abrantes, the invader and occupier of Portugal.

Shako of an officer of Hussars.

Infantry

1st Regt. (Col. Casimir Malachowski), 2,690 men; *2nd Regt.* (Col. Stanislas Potocki), 3,030; *3rd Regt.* (Col. Edouard Zoltowski), 2,647; *4th Regt.* (Col. Wierzbinski), 2,241 – two battalions in Spain; *5th Regt.* (Col. Prince Michel Radziwill), 2,104; *6th Regt.* (Col. Julian Sierawski), 2,673; *7th Regt.* (Col. Jakubowicz), 1,095 – two battalions in Spain; *8th Regt.* (Col. Stuart), 2,302; *9th Regt.* (Col. Prince Antoine Sulkowski), 2,050 – two battalions in Spain; *10th Regt.* (Col. Downarowicz), 1,996 – two battalions in Danzig; *11th Regt.* (Col. Mielzynski), 2,145 – two battalions in Danzig; *12th Regt.* (Col. Weyssenhof), 2,604. *Total* 28,387 men.

Cavalry

1st Chasseurs (Col. Przebendowski), 937 men; *2nd Lancers* (Col. Tyszkiewicz), 1,163; *3rd Lancers* (Col. Lonczynski), 1,015; *4th Chasseurs* (Col. Kwasniewski), 687 – in Germany; *5th Chasseurs* (Col. Cas Turno), 1,097; *6th Lancers* (Col. Dom Dziewanowski), 1,099. *Total* 5,998 men. Artillery, Engineers and Train, *total* 2,620 men. *Grand Total*, 37,005 men.

FRANCO-GALICIAN ARMY

Infantry

1st Regt. (Col. Szneider), 3,425 men; *2nd Regt.* (Col. Siemionowski), 2,852; *3rd Regt.* (Col. Miaskowski), 3,422; *4th Regt.* (Col. Kenczycki), 2,338; *5th Regt.* (Col. Prince Constantin Czartoryski), 2,561; *6th Regt.* (Col. Hornowski), 1,985. *Total* 16,583 men. The 4th Regiment was later disbanded, and the 1st, 2nd, 3rd, 5th and 6th became the Polish 13th to 17th Regiments respectively.

Cavalry

1st Lancers (Col. Zawadzki), 840 men; *2nd Lancers* (Col. Rozwadowski), 954; *3rd Lancers* (Col. Przysychowski), 936; *4th Lancers* (Col. Potocki), 899; *5th Lancers* (Col. Ryszczewski), 943; *6th Lancers* (Col. Trzeciecki), 916; *7th Lancers* (Col. Tarnowski), 661; *8th Hussars* (Col. Tolinski), 1,049; *9th Hussars* (Col. Uminski), 803; *10th Kürassiers* (Col. Malachowski), 610. These units later became the 7th to 16th Polish cavalry regiments.

Grand Total Franco-Galician troops: 25,193 men. *Grand Total Polish forces:* 62,198 men. *Detached forces:* Spain – 6,265 men; Danzig – 3,024 men; Germany – 686 men.

In May 1809 Poniatowski created a company of Guides from Galician noble families, comprising four officers, twelve N.C.O.s, two trumpeters and sixty soldiers.

It may be added that the Chevau-légers of the French Imperial Guard were present at the Battle of Wagram (5–6 July 1809), and overthrew the Austrian Schwarzenberg Uhlans in one charge.

Russian troops moved against the Austrians in Warsaw on the same day, in support of the Poles; but this support was limited and uncoordinated, and Poniatowski was forced on to the defensive again in the second week of June. A second Austrian assault on Sandomir failed bloodily on 15 June, but on the 18th the garrison was forced to capitulate – with full honours – through lack of ammunition. Meanwhile Poniatowski's forces were growing in strength, reaching a total of some 24,000 through the raising of six new infantry and ten cavalry regiments in Galicia. Krakow was retaken from the Austrians on 14 July; and two days later news of the armistice of Znaim between Austria and France reached Krakow, ending the campaign. The subsequent Treaty of Schönbrunn brought to the duchy west Galicia, the area surrounding Krakow, and the area of Zamosc.

The army of the Duchy of Warsaw, including the new 'Franco-Galician' formations raised dur-

Russia 1812

The scope of this campaign was so vast, and the contribution of the Polish units so widespread, that for reasons of space it is impossible to go into details in this book. A summary of units engaged, and a brief list of some of their most notable actions must suffice.

At the beginning of March 1812 Prince Poniatowski, C.-in-C. of the army of the Duchy of Warsaw, received orders from the Emperor to prepare to march. With the absorption of the Franco-Galician units, the forces of the duchy now totalled 74,700 men, 22,850 horses and 165 cannon. The entire V Corps of the Grande Armée was composed of Polish troops, organized as follows:

Corps Commander: Prince Poniatowski; *Chief of Staff*, Gen. Fiszer; *Deputy Chief of Staff*, Gen. Rautenstrauch.

16th Division: Commander, Gen. Zajonczek; Chief of Staff, Col. Weyssenhoff; Brigade Commanders, Gens. Mielzinski and Paszkowski. 3rd, 15th and 16th Infantry Regiments; 19th Light Cavalry Brigade (Gen. Tyskiewicz); 4th Chasseurs; 12th Lancers.

17th Division: Commander, Gen. Dombrowski; Chief of Staff, Col. Cedrowski; Brigade Commanders, Gens. Axamitowski and Piotorwski. 1st, 6th, 14th and 17th Infantry Regiments; Light Cavalry Brigade (Gen. Dziewanowski); 1st Chasseurs.

18th Division: Commander, Gen. Kniaziewicz; Chief of Staff, Col. Nowicki; Brigade Commanders, Gens. Bieganski and Grabowski. 2nd, 8th and 12th Infantry Regiments; 20th Light Cavalry Brigade (Gen. Prince Antoine Sulkowski); 5th Chasseurs and 13th Hussars; Light Cavalry Brigade (Gen. Niemojewski); 6th and 8th Lancers; Light Cavalry Brigade (Gen. Axamitowski); 10th Hussars.

4th Polish Light Cavalry Division: Commander, Gen. Rozniecki. 28th Light Cavalry Brigade (Gen. Dziewarowski); 2nd and 11th Lancers; 29th Light Cavalry Brigade (Gen. Turno); 3rd and 16th Lancers. Under command, 14th Polish Kürassiers.

In addition to these formations, the 4th, 7th and 9th Polish Infantry Regiments were attached to

Field-Marshal Barclay de Tolly, commander of Russia's two western armies at the outset of the 1812 campaign.

Girard's division of IX Corps; and Prince Michael Radziwill's brigade (5th, 10th and 11th Polish Infantry) were in Danzig as part of Macdonald's X Corps. The Legion of the Vistula, in two brigades consisting of the 1st and 3rd Regiments and the 2nd and 4th Regiments, served in Claparede's division of the Young Guard under Mortier. In August 1812 a brigade formed from the 13th Infantry and a regiment of the National Guard of Warsaw, commanded by General Kwasniewski, joined a Saxon division in Reynier's VII Corps.

The Russian General Wittgenstein.

Marshal Bernadotte, who succeeded to the crown of Sweden; in 1813 he led troops against his former master, Napoleon.

On 23 June 1812 the Grande Armée crossed the Niemen on to Russian soil; for months beforehand the Duchy of Warsaw had been a vast camp and assembly area, and the population were no doubt heartily glad to be rid of some of their guests. Few, indeed, would pass that way again. The army ran into difficulties straight away: although the Russians retreated before them, they poisoned the wells and streams and removed or destroyed all grain. Hundreds of men died from heat prostration every day, and the young Polish conscripts suffered particularly badly. The poor forage available soon began to kill off cavalry mounts in thousands. On 23 June V Corps numbered 30,000 men; by 28 July it mustered only 22,000, although no major actions had yet been fought.

On 27 June the Poles entered Wilna, Lithuania – a Polish possession until 1795 – and were welcomed as liberators. In response to local requests a federation of Lithuania with the duchy was proclaimed on 1 July, and the raising of five infantry and four lancer regiments was put in hand. These were designated the 18th to 22nd Infantry and 17th to 20th Cavalry Regiments of the army of the duchy – although they never reached full strength, and most of them perished in the horror of the Russian winter. Napoleon also formed a guard of honour from young Lithuanian nobles which became the 3rd Chevau-légers Lanciers de la Garde.

On 9 July at Mir, on 10 July at Koralice and on 14 July at Nieswiez, the Polish cavalry were roughly handled by Russian forces among whom Platow's Cossacks were prominent. The Poles took some measure of revenge on 25 July, when the 6th and 10th Cavalry smashed the Russian Ingermannland Dragoons. On 13 August the Polish 17th Division and the 2nd, 7th and 15th Lancers were detached to act as a link with Saxon and Austrian forces on the southern flank of the army, leaving V Corps with but 15,000 men. On 16 August the Poles were heavily committed to bitter fighting at Smolensk, with more than 2,000 casualties, including four generals and sixty officers. Late in August the first elements of the new Lithuanian infantry regiments arrived with the 17th Division; at about the same time Victor sent the 4th, 7th and 9th Polish Infantry Regiments to

Minsk. At Borodino on 5–7 September the Poles were again heavily engaged. On 5 September Poniatowski led the bulk of the Polish units forward on the right flank of the army, where they took the Schweradino redoubt. On 7 September a further flanking movement developed on the right, and the Polish infantry fought around the village of Uticza; the cavalry were also active in this sector, taking Pasarzew. The Vistula Legion fought on the left flank under Claparede.

In the second half of the month, while Napoleon occupied the smoking ruins of Moscow and brooded on his dilemma, the Polish corps was sent to clear strong Russian forces threatening the lines of communication. They fought at Podolsk on 24 September, then following the enemy as he fell back towards Kaluga, fighting several further actions. Losses had been extremely heavy, and the Polish infantry regiments were now reorganized with two battalions each instead of three. At about this time the Vistula Legion joined the other Polish units.

The lull in operations between late September and mid-October ended on 18 October, when heavy Russian pressure developed against Murat's outposts; the King of Naples was forced to withdraw inside a Polish infantry square. By the time they had fought their way back to Woronowo the Poles had lost another 500 dead (including General Fiszer) and 1,000 wounded (including Prince Anton Sulkowski), and the V Corps was down to 12,000 men. On 18/19 October the retreat from Moscow began. Its miseries have been chronicled too often to merit repetition here; suffice it to say that the Polish troops suffered as badly as any element in the dwindling and wretched army. After fighting at Borowsk and Wiasma, V Corps – so-called – had but 800 effectives under arms. The Vistula Legion, which had joined the Grande Armée 7,000 strong, was reduced to 1,500 by the time the army reached Smolensk on 9 November. The 3rd (Lithuanian) Lancers of the Guard were wiped out at Slonim on 3 November. The detached 17th Division under Dombrowski was still 4,000 strong, but it suffered heavily at Borissow on the Beresina while vainly trying to save the vital bridge from Tschernichew's Russians. While the ghost of the Grande Armée straggled across the two rickety

Berthier, Napoleon's invaluable chief of staff.

bridges which were improvised at Studienka on 27 November, the now-reunited V Corps under Zajonczek held off a Russian advance up the west bank of the Beresina. Poniatowski, who was sick and travelling in a carriage, only escaped across the river with difficulty. Command of V Corps passed rapidly from Zajonczek to Kniaziewicz to Krasinski, as the generals were wounded one by one. On the night of 6 November the Polish Lancers of the Guard and the 7th Polish Lancers escorted Napoleon as he deserted the rabble of his army. On 9 November the remains of V Corps crossed the Niemen and entered their homeland once again. Poniatowski reviewed them at Warsaw on Christmas Day; apart from Dombrowski's 17th Division, they numbered 400 men – but they still had their eagles and forty cannon.

The passage of the River Niemen on 24 June 1812, at the start of the fateful Russian campaign.

The Last Act

The Russians flooded into the Duchy of Warsaw in the early months of 1813; they occupied the city on 9 February, and Poniatowski began the painful business of reorganizing his forces from Krakow. Elements of Polish units were scattered all over northern Europe, and it was not until the victory of Lützen brought a brief respite with the armistice of Pleisswitz that a Polish corps could be assembled. By this time the Russian advance had pushed Poniatowski back to Zittau in Saxony. From composite units of survivors, raw conscripts, renumbered regiments, returned prisoners and other 'odds and ends', Napoleon and Poniatowski created VIII Corps, as follows:

26th Infantry Division (Gen. Kamieniecki): *1st Brigade* (Gen. Sierawski), 1st and 16th Infantry Regiments; *2nd Brigade* (Gen. Malachowski), 8th and 15th Infantry Regiments.
27th Infantry Division (Gen. Krasinski): *1st Brigade* (Gen. Grabowski) 12th Infantry Regiment; *2nd Brigade* (Gen. Lonczynski) 2nd and 14th Infantry Regiments (ex-Dombrowski's division).

The cavalry became the 4th Reserve Cavalry Corps under General Kellerman, Comte de Valmy, as follows:

Advanced Guard (Gen. Uminski): 14th Kürassiers (Col. Dziekonski); Krakus (Maj. Rzuchowski). *8th Light Cavalry Division* (Gen. Prince Sulkowski): 1st, 3rd and 6th Chasseurs, in two brigades commanded by Gens. Weyssenhof and Turno. *7th Light Cavalry Division* (Gen. Sokolnicki): 8th and 16th Lancers and 13th Hussars in two brigades commanded by Gens. Tolinski and Kwasniewski.

The 2nd and 4th Cavalry, ex-Dombrowski's division, were brigaded under General Krukowiecki and attached to VIII Corps. Various isolated Polish regiments were still in existence in Danzig, Zamosc, Modlin and Hamburg. At Wittemberg were two regiments now in French pay: the Regiment of the Vistula, a two-battalion remnant of the old Legion, and the '4e Régiment Polonaise', a composite of the old 4th, 7th and 9th Infantry. Note that many of the units of VIII Corps, above, bore no direct relationship to the pre-1813 regiments of the same numerical designation.

After the victory of Dresden (26 August 1813) the release of Polish prisoners brought VIII Corps' strength up to 12,000. The new formation was blooded at Katzbach on 26 August. Krukowiecki's cavalry brigade – 2nd and 4th Regiments – distinguished themselves at Dennewitz on 6 September. On 16 October there opened the last great battle of Napoleon's Polish allies – Leipzig, the Battle of the Nations. At first based at Mark-Kleeburg, the 9,000 Poles were pushed back to Dölitz by an attack by 18,000 Russians and Prussians under Kleist. That night Poniatowski was nominated Marshal of France. The Poles remained at Dölitz throughout 17 October, apart from elements which held the suburb of Hallé and areas to the north. The city had become a trap in the middle of a ring of converging Allied armies, a trap with only one way out – a single bridge over the Elster. The heavy trains were sent out over the bridge on the night of 17–18 October; it was then prepared for eventual demolition. On 18 October the Allies renewed their assaults, and bitter fighting took place. That night Napoleon ordered the evacuation of the city, and during the following day conditions within the areas of French occupation deteriorated as the rearguard formations tried to fight off the Allied pressure and panic began to infect those units which had not yet managed to withdraw over the bridge. When the Russians forced their way into the city, after bloody fighting in which the Poles played a desperate part, chaos gripped the bridgehead – and at that point the Elster bridge was prematurely blown, leaving 20,000 French, German and Polish troops trapped in Leipzig. Among them were Poniatowski and the remnants of VIII Corps. Most fell into enemy hands; many attempted to swim to safety across the Elster, and were drowned. Among these latter was Marshal Prince Poniatowski – and with him

died, for all practical purposes, the Grand Duchy of Warsaw.

One by one, isolated fortresses all over northern Germany capitulated, and many Poles were among the garrisons. Those few thousands who remained with the French forces as they retreated towards France were only kept in the ranks with great difficulty after the news of Poniatowski's death spread. Eventually, and in violation of a promise made to Dombrowski, Napoleon ordered the incorporation of all Polish units into the French Army. Isolated units, inspired by personal loyalty to the Emperor, distinguished themselves during the French campaign of 1814.

The Treaty of Paris was signed on 11 April 1814, and the war was over. Napoleon became ruler of Elba and was permitted to take with him a battalion of grenadiers of the Guard and a squadron of 120 men of the Polish Chevau-légers of the Guard. This squadron was formed completely of volunteers and was commanded by Jermanowski. Article 19 of the Treaty of Paris

The Prussian General Kleist von Nollendorff.

The capture of General Vandamme by Cossacks on 30 August 1813, after the Battle of Kulm.

defined the future position of the Poles who had fought so valiantly for so long for the Emperor:

'Polish troops of all arms are at liberty to return to their homelands having terminated their honourable service.

'Officers, N.C.O.s and men may retain the decorations which they have been awarded and will continue to receive the pensions attached to these decorations.'

The Hundred Days
At the beginning of April 1815 it was decreed that five foreign regiments should be formed for service with Napoleon's army. The 3rd Foreign Regiment was formed of Poles under Majors Szulc and Goloszewski. The men came mainly from the old Legion of the Vistula. The Elba Squadron of Polish Cavalry became the 1st Squadron of the Regiment of Chevau-légers Lanciers de la Garde, and fought well at Waterloo. On 1 October 1815 this squadron passed into Russian service in the new kingdom of Poland.

Uniforms

Infantry
At the beginning of 1807 the infantry wore dark blue kurtkas with crimson facings; black felt czapka decorated with a brass sun-burst plate, dark blue or white trousers, brown greatcoat. Plume, pompon, epaulettes and cords as follows: grenadiers red; voltigeurs yellow; fusiliers light blue.

This uniform was modified by a decree of 2 March 1807 as follows (all kurtkas dark blue): *1st Division:* Lapels yellow, collar and cuffs red, yellow buttons bearing the regimental number; trousers worn over boots, closed at the bottoms with eight buttons and eight loops. On duty officers wore gilt gorgets with silver eagles; gilt belt with silver eagle. Field officers wore dark blue

1 Driver, Military Train
2 Port-aigle, Grenadier Company, 5th
  Infantry Regiment, 1810–14
3 Aigle Guard

MICHAEL ROFFE

A

**Trumpeter, 14th Kürassiers,
parade dress**

B

Trumpeter, Horse Artillery, full dress

C

1 Officer, Horse Artillery, full dress
2 Voltigeur Cornet, Legion of the
  Vistula, 1808
3 Trumpeter, 5th Chasseurs à
  Cheval, parade dress

D

1 Drum Major, 1st Infantry Regiment
2 Voltigeur sergeant, 4th Infantry Regiment, 1810–14
3 Trooper, 14th Kürassiers, parade dress, 1807–14

MICHAEL ROFFE

E

1 **Tambour of Fusiliers, 4th Infantry Regiment, field service marching order, 1809**
2 **Sous-lieutenant, 13th Hussars, full dress, 1806–14**
3 **Grenadier, 13th Infantry Regiment, 1809–14**

F

1 **Gunner, Horse Artillery, stable dress**
2 **Trooper, Lancers, stable dress**
3 **Trooper, Kürassiers, stable dress**

MICHAEL ROFFE

G

1 Brigadier-Trompette, Chevau-légers Polonais de la Garde, marching order, 1810–14

2 Officer, Krakus, 1812

3 Trooper, Lithuanian Tartars of the Guard, 1812

Cossacks in combat. The Polish corps was harassed from the earliest stages of the Russian campaign by Cossack attacks, and at first the Polish cavalry made a rather undistinguished showing.

and gold silk sashes; junior officers, white leather belts. Degen with steel grip. *2nd Division:* Crimson lapels, collar and cuffs, white buttons and cap-plates: otherwise as 1st Division. *3rd Division:* Lapels, collar and cuffs white, yellow buttons and cap-plate, otherwise as 1st Division. In undress, officers wore dark blue frock-coats with collars of the same colour, and bicorns.

The cockade was white like that of the ancient Polish republic. Napoleon imposed the French cockade on the Franco-Polish regiments in 1809, but Prince Poniatowski reintroduced the white cockade when these troops were incorporated into the army of the Duchy of Warsaw on 1 January 1810.

In the decree of 3 September 1810 it was directed that all regiments of infantry would wear the same facings.

Officers' Full Dress: Dark blue coat, white waistcoat and trousers; collar closed and piped in crimson (voltigeurs – yellow unpiped collars). White lapels, straight cuffs with crimson flaps and white piping. The coat was closed by means of hooks and open on the thighs. Horizontal, three-pointed pocket flaps with crimson piping. The skirts were hooked back to show the white lining with, in the corners, embroidered hunting horns for the voltigeurs, stars for the fusiliers and grenades for the grenadiers. Yellow metal buttons bearing in relief the number of the regiment. Seven small buttons on each side of the lapels, three large buttons below on the left side and three buttonholes on the right. Two large buttons in the small of the back, three on each pocket and one small button for each epaulette. The waistcoat showed beneath the coat and was closed with small buttons; three on each pocket. Long breeches, Hungarian boots. Black stock edged in white. Black bicorn edged in black silk; on the left a double loop of gold half an inch wide (held by a gold button) which fixed the cockade. *Grenadiers:* Officers wear bearskins with red plumes and silver cords. The bearskin is of the same pattern as those of the men. *Voltigeurs:* Officers wear a hat with a

A flag of the 4th Battalion, 7th Infantry Regiment, captured at Wiasma in 1812.

yellow pompon fourteen centimetres high. *Fusilier:* Officers have a black pompon above the cockade. *Officers' Undress:* Dark blue frock-coat with similar collar and lapels, closed with nine large buttons. Dark blue trousers. Grenadier officers have a red hat pompon. *Surtout:* Dark blue with seven large buttons on each lapel; under this, waistcoat and trousers of white dimity or nankeen as desired.

N.C.O.s and Soldiers: Dark blue coat, white lapels buttoned back and closed with hooks; below the plastron the kurtka is closed with two large buttons. Dark blue trousers for everyday wear, white for parades, the latter worn with white gaiters under them. *Grenadiers:* Bearskin bonnet (mostly shown with a small black peak edged in yellow metal) leaning slightly forward. Brass plate with white metal eagle and bearing the number of the regiment between two flanking grenades. Top of the bearskin red with a white cross, red cords and plume. Long moustaches are worn. Red epaulettes. *Voltigeurs:* Shako with yellow cords, above the cockade a yellow and green plume.

Short moustaches are worn. Green epaulettes. *Fusiliers:* Czapka of black felt, nine inches high and ten inches square, white metal eagle above a yellow metal plate bearing the regimental number. Black leather peak edged in brass. Above the eagle a white cockade surmounted by a black pompon. White cords, terminating in tassels which are silver and crimson for N.C.O.s. White leather work. Dark blue shoulder-straps. The fusiliers were clean-shaven. Black leather pouch with a regimental number in brass for the fusiliers, number within a hunting horn for voltigeurs and number and a grenade for the grenadiers. Dark blue forage cap with red piping and tassel. On the march, the forage cap was carried rolled up under the pouch and the plume (in its case) was strapped to the sabre sheath. White waistcoat for fatigues (collar, cuffs and piping crimson?), grey greatcoat. *Sappeurs:* Grenadier's bearskin; on the upper arms of the kurtka a badge of two crossed axes with a grenade in red cloth. White leather apron, wide white bandolier and black pouch for the axe, small pouch with the sappeur's badge, gauntlets. The sabre has a brass grip terminating in a cock's head and dragoon carbines are carried. Sappeurs wore full beards. *Musicians:* Drummers and musicians wore a great variety of dress following the whim of their commander.

Badges of Rank

Officers (indicated by epaulettes): *Colonel* – two epaulettes with bullion fringes, no embroidery on the straps. *Major* – the same epaulettes but with the top in silver. *Lieutenant-colonel* – on the left an epaulette with bullion fringes, on the right a contre-epaulette without fringes. *Captain* – on the left a fringed epaulette, on the right a contre-epaulette. *Lieutenant* – as for a captain, but with a line of crimson, one-eighth of an inch wide along the straps. *Sous-lieutenant* – the same epaulettes, but with two lines of crimson silk zigzagging along the straps. *Adjutant-major* – on the right a fringed epaulette, on the left a contre-epaulette. Epaulettes were gold for all infantry officers, the *porte-épée* and hat cords silver, the gorget gold with a silver Polish eagle. *N.C.O.s: Corporal* – two stripes of yellow cloth two inches above the cuffs. *Sergeant* – one gold stripe on each arm and one on the strap of the epaulette or shoulder-strap. *Sergeant-*

Field-Marshal Kutusov, Napoleon's opponent at Borodino – a relatively flattering portrait.

major – two gold stripes. *Fourrier* – one gold chevron four inches above the elbow. All N.C.O.s have a gold top band one inch wide to their shakos or czapkas.

Armament

All fusilier officers carry French-pattern Degen with gilt plate and grip; black sheath, leather belt. Mounted officers carry sabres with yellow grips and sheaths, trimmed in black leather; silver spurs. Grenadier and voltigeur officers also carry sabres. N.C.O.s, grenadiers and voltigeurs carry sabres as well as muskets and bayonets, the fusiliers only the musket and bayonet.

Foot Artillery

Officers' Full Dress: Dark green coat; collar, lapels and cuffs black velvet with red edging; white waistcoat and trousers; yellow metal buttons bearing in relief a flaming grenade above crossed cannon barrels. Style of coat, number of buttons, hooks, stock, hat and cockade as for officers of infantry. At the turnback corners, gold embroidered flaming grenades. Riding boots, silver spurs, gilt fittings and buckles. *Undress:* Dark green, single-breasted frock-coat, black velvet collar and cuffs with red piping. Black or green trousers. Cut as for the infantry. *Surtout:* As for undress, but double-breasted with seven large buttons on each lapel. Below this, waistcoat and trousers of white dimity or nankeen according to choice.

N.C.O.s and Gunners: Dark green kurtka with black collar, lapels and cuffs piped in red. Green trousers or white trousers and gaiters. Red epaulettes. Shako with yellow chin scales and yellow metal plate bearing a flaming grenade and two crossed cannon barrels, all surmounted by a white metal eagle. Red cords, pompon and plume. *Veste de corvée (Fatigue jacket):* White with green collar and cuffs and green piping round the pockets. *Forage Cap:* Dark green edged in yellow. *Conducteurs (Drivers):* Grey/blue kurtkas with grey trousers (with leather insets); dark blue czapka trimmed with black astrakhan. On the left upper arm an oval brass plate bearing the number of the vehicle and of the division. *Badges of Rank:* As for the infantry. *Armament:* As for the infantry except that N.C.O.s and men have dragoon carbines and sabres with red straps. *Train d'équipage:* Dress as for the artillery, but the kurtka is blue/grey with light yellow collar and cuffs. Buttons, epaulettes, etc., are white.

Kürassiers

Full Dress: Dark blue coat faced in red, red collar closed with three hooks, square red cuffs with dark blue piping. Two grenades in the turnback corners, pockets in the folds of the skirt. The coat closed by nine buttons and the skirt projected nine inches below the kürass. Three buttons on each pocket, two at the rear of the waist and one for each epaulette. The buttons are flat and yellow and bear in relief the number of the regiment. White waistcoat not visible beneath the coat; white leather breeches closing with four buttons below the knee, white cloth knee-cuffs reaching to four inches above the knee and closing with four buttons. Cuffed boots rising to three inches above the knee, long, buckle-on steel spurs. Steel kürass with front and back plate with brass rivets, leather

The crossing of the Beresina in November 1812; the remnants of the Grande Armée attempt to save themselves. The Polish Corps, reduced to a few hundred men, fought gallantly on the retreat.

straps covered in brass scales. The kürass is edged with red cloth three inches wide the outer edge of which has a silver edging one inch wide. French-style helmet with red plume on the left side (steel body, brass combe, horse-hair crest and tuft, yellow chin scales, black fur turban extending over peak, which is edged in brass. No neck shield). Black stock edged in white, white leather gauntlets with cuffs seven inches high.

Undress: Dark blue frock-coat faced in red and closed by nine yellow buttons. Red collar closed with three hooks. Pointed cuffs outlined in red piping and closed with three small buttons. Grenades on the turnbacks; vertical pockets with three points edged in red piping. Plain dark blue trousers, same boots as for full dress. Bicorn as for the Chasseurs à Cheval with red plume. *Surtout:* Dark blue with similar collar and cuffs, pockets in the folds of the skirt; seven buttons on each lapel. *Greatcoat:* White cloth, closed collar with yellow metal loops and red piping; circular cape collar (*rotonde*) nine inches high. Red lining twelve inches wide.

N.C.O.s and soldiers have the same uniform as the officers, according to regulations.

Badges of Rank: Gold epaulettes as for infantry officers; *porte-épée* one and a half inches wide terminating in a silver tassel (bullion fringes for field officers). *Armament:* French model Pallasch with yellow hilt, polished steel sheath; steel fitted pistols. White leatherwork with yellow metal fittings. White leather bandolier with yellow buckle worn over the kürass.

Chasseurs à Cheval
Full Dress: Dark green kurtka lined in dark green, collar closed with three hooks, pointed cuffs. Seams on the rear of the coat one inch wide, pockets in the folds. The kurtka is closed with nine round brass buttons and there are two on each pocket. Long breeches with a double side-stripe of one-inch-wide braid in the facing colour. The breeches close at the bottoms with six hooks and one button covered in green cloth. Black leather instep straps. Collar, cuffs and piping in the regimental facing colour. White waistcoat under the kurtka. The élite company and the officers wear busbies; the bag of the busby is in the facing colour and the top lining is gathered under a large central gold button. Black stock edged white.

Battle of Lützen, or Gross-Görschen, 2 May 1813.

White gauntlets for officers, gloves for the men. Short boots under the breeches; yellow metal screw-in spurs.

Undress: Dark green frock-coat with dark green lining; collar closed with three hooks; pointed cuffs in the collar colour closed with two buttons. Coat closed with nine buttons in yellow metal. Vertical pockets in the skirts, trident shaped with three buttons. The skirts hooked back to form turnbacks, gold hunting horns embroidered in the turnback corners. French-style white breeches or dark green breeches, Hungarian boots edged in black with a small tassel in the front. Breeches for everyday wear in dark green or grey cloth, fitted inside the legs with black leather and on the left thigh to guard against wear from the sabre. Black bicorn with a two-inch-wide black binding and on the left side a double gold braid loop and a gold button holding the cockade. *Surtout:* Dark green as are the collar and cuffs, seven yellow buttons on each lapel; vertical pockets in the rear skirts. *Greatcoat:* White cloth, high collar (with piping in the facing colour) closed by three small buttons; the cape collar could be removed.

N.C.O.s and soldiers wear the same uniform as for the officers' full dress. The élite company wear busbies with red plumes and cords, the centre companies have shakos with white cords. White leatherwork, yellow scale epaulettes with, for the élite company, red fringes, for the other companies, white fringes.

The regimental facing colours were: 1st Regiment: red; 4th Regiment: crimson; 5th Regiment: orange. The trumpeters rode greys and wore white busbies with yellow and green cords, white kurtkas with waistcoat *à la Hussarde* with braid in the regimental facing colour. Trumpet cords silver and crimson.

Badges of Rank: As for the infantry except that the strap of the epaulette is covered in yellow metal scales; *porte-épée* of woven black leather with silver tassel; silver cords and gold pompon to busby. N.C.O.s and soldiers are distinguished in the following manner: *Corporal* – two stripes of yellow cloth, edged in red, placed two inches above the cuff. *Sergeant* – one silver stripe, edged in red, in the same position. *Sergeant-major* – two silver stripes edged in red as above. *Fourrier* – one gold chevron edged in red.

Armament: Sabre with yellow metal hilt, steel

Contemporary engraving of the Battle of Dresden, 26 August 1813.

sheath with yellow fittings. Black pouch decorated in gold with the number of the regiment between two wreaths. Bandolier of black polished leather three inches wide bordered with two gold laces half an inch wide. Yellow metal buckle. Black leather belt two inches wide with gold decoration, slings one inch wide. For everyday wear the officers wore white polished leather bandoliers.

For the 2nd, 3rd and 16th Regiments the lance pennons are red over white. For the 7th and 16th Regiments (Franco-Galician) the lance pennons are in three colours, the triangular part which is attached to the staff being blue, the top fly being red and the bottom fly white. The 17th to 21st Regiments (Lithuanian) have blue over white lance pennons.

Trumpeters' dress was extremely varied and at the discretion of the commander. Generally they wore white busbies and kurtkas, red plumes and rode greys. N.C.O.s and soldiers wore the same dress as the officers except that their greatcoats were white with collars in the facing colour.

Badges of Rank: As for the Chasseurs à Cheval.
Armament: French-style light cavalry sabre with yellow three-bar hilt, steel sheath and fittings.

Yellow fitted pistols. Bandolier as for the Chasseurs à Cheval. Black leather belt three inches wide with a half-inch-wide border along each edge, yellow buckle-plate with the Polish eagle. The belt is worn over the buttoned kurtka.

Lancers
Full Dress: Dark blue kurtka of Polish cut, dark blue lining. Collar closed with three hooks, pointed cuffs. The kurtka closes by means of hooks. Vertical pockets in the rear skirts. Piping to lapels, cuffs and along seams on the rear of the jacket and the sleeves. Flat yellow metal buttons bearing the regimental number – seven on each lapel, three on each pocket, two at the rear waist and two for the epaulettes. White waistcoat under the kurtka. Long dark blue breeches worn over the boots with double bands down each leg in the facing colour, each band half an inch wide. These breeches close with six hooks and one button at the base of the leg in the facing colour. Black leather instep straps. Black czapka nine inches high and each top edge ten inches long. The top part is separated from the round bottom part by a two-inch-wide gold lace band. Each corner

DER RHEINISCHE COURIER

verliehrt auf der Heimreise von der Leipziger Meße alles.

A contemporary cartoon depicting Napoleon's plight after the defeat of Leipzig in October 1813. The caption reads 'The Rhenish Courier, on the way home from the Leipzig Fair, loses everything'.

of the top part has a metal cap with a hook for the cords. On the left-hand top side (in the middle of that side) is the white Polish cockade under a gold Maltese cross. In the front, over the lace band, a gilt plate bearing the number of the regiment in relief. Black leather peak edged in yellow metal, yellow chin scales, black plume fifteen inches high for junior officers, white plumes for field officers. Short boots with yellow screw-in spurs. White gloves. Black stock edged white.

Undress: Dark blue frock-coat lined in the same colour and closed with nine semi-round, yellow buttons. Collar closed by three hooks. Pointed cuffs, with piping, closed by two small buttons; vertical, trident-shaped pocket flaps. Skirts hooked together at the bottom. Hungarian breeches and polished boots. Black bicorn. *Surtout:* Same cloth as above, seven buttons (yellow, half-round) on each lapel. *Greatcoat:* Dark blue cloth, high collar and cape collar reaching to the waist-belt.

Regiments of lancers are distinguished by their buttons (which bear their number) and by their facing colour worn on collar, lapels, cuffs, trouser stripes and piping as shown below.

Regiment	Collar	Collar piping	Lapels	Lapel piping	Cuffs	Cuff piping	Trouser stripes
2	Red	White		Yellow	Red	White	Yellow
3	Crimson	White		White	Crimson	White	Yellow
6	White	Crimson	Dark	Crimson	Crimson	White	Crimson
7	Yellow	Red	blue	Red	Yellow	Red	Yellow
8	Red	Red		Red	Yellow	Red	Red
9	Red	Blue		White	Dark blue	White	Red
11		White	Crimson	White	Dark blue	White	Crimson
12		White	Dark blue	White	Dark blue	White	Crimson
15	Crimson	White	Crimson	White	Crimson	White	Crimson
16		White	Dark blue	Crimson	Crimson	White	Crimson
17		White	Dark blue	Crimson	Crimson	White	Crimson
18	Crimson	White	Dark blue	Crimson	Crimson	White	Crimson
19	Yellow	Yellow	Yellow	Yellow	Yellow	Yellow	Yellow
20	Yellow	Yellow	Yellow	Yellow	Yellow	Yellow	Yellow
21	Orange	Orange	Orange	Orange	Orange	Orange	Orange

Hussars

Dark blue pelisse (Metyk) lined with white fur and edged in black fur with three rows each of eighteen to twenty buttons according to the wearer's size; a dolman with crimson collar and the same number of buttons; Hungarian sash with five sets of knots; Hungarian breeches with thigh knots; a sleeved waistcoat for forage duties and long grey breeches, reinforced with leather and closing at the bottom with six buttons. Polished Hungarian boots with steel spurs. Light blue shako with cords. *Officers' Full Dress:* Pelisse lined in crimson cloth and edged with white astrakhan; five rows each of eighteen to twenty buttons with silver lacing. The pelisse is edged with lace and has lace decoration to the rear. Crimson dolman, same lace, buttons and ornaments as the pelisse. Light blue breeches with thigh knots; Hungarian boots with lace trim and tassel. Hungarian sash in silver and crimson. Light blue shako with silver cords and decoration according to rank. *Undress* (for summer): Dark blue dolman, crimson collar edged with lace; five rows of lace, three rows each of five buttons, otherwise as for full dress. White waistcoat, long, grey breeches fitted with grey leather inserts, crimson side-stripes each having six white buttons. For winter a dark blue pelisse edged in white astrakhan with five rows of silver and crimson lace. Light blue forage cap with silver piping as for the French Army. White greatcoat.

N.C.O.s and Soldiers: Light blue shakos and their pelisses are trimmed with black lamb's-wool. Trumpeters wear red fox fur busbies, white pelisses edged in red fox fur and having white and crimson lacing. The trumpeters of the 10th

The French garrison of Spandau is escorted into captivity in 1813 by Prussian and Russian troops.

Hussars had a blue dolman, crimson breeches and yellow boots; those of the 13th Hussars a crimson dolman, blue breeches and red boots. The officers and men of the élite company wore black astrakhan busbies with light blue bags held by a large light blue button. The 10th Hussars had gold lace, decorations, buttons, stripes, etc., but their shako cords remained silver, their pelisses were edged in black astrakhan and their shakos were light blue. (The 13th Hussars were as described in the main body of the text.)

Badges of Rank: Officers were distinguished by the number of chevrons over the cuff: *Sous-lieutenant* – one; *Lieutenant* – two; *Capitaine* – three; *Chef d'escadron* – four; *Major* – five (one in gold and four in silver for the 13th Hussars or one in silver and four in gold for the 10th Hussars); *Colonel* – five chevrons in silver or gold according to regiment. *Porte-épée* of woven black leather with silver or gold tassel (heavy bullions for field officers). *Armament:* Steel basket-hilted sabre and sheath,

silver-fitted pistols, black leather bandolier with eagle and small silver edging, black leather sabretache bearing a silver eagle (officers have gold crown, gold regimental number below the eagle and gold lace edging). Belt, slings, etc., of black leather with silver buckles.

Horse Artillery

Full Dress: Dark green kurtka of the same cut as for the Chasseurs and lined in dark green. Black velvet collar four inches high, piped in red and closed with four hooks. Gold grenades embroidered on each side of the collar. Pointed black velvet cuffs piped in red and closed with two small buttons. The kurtka is piped in red and closed with eight gold buttons. The skirts are nine inches long and decorated with embroidered gold grenades. There are two buttons at the bottom of the turnbacks, two at the rear waist and two on the shoulders. The buttons are yellow and semi-round. Long dark green breeches worn over the boots with black velvet side-stripes two inches wide piped in red. The breeches close at the ankles with seven hooks and one black velvet button at the bottom. Black velvet waistcoat with gold braid and buttons. Short boots with steel, screw-in spurs. Black gauntlets. Black fur busby ten inches high and larger at the top than at the bottom; dark green bag held by a gold button. Gold lion's-head bosses, gold chin scales and cords, and pompon above the cockade with two small silver cords and tassels.

Undress: Coat of dark green cloth with similar lining; lapels with rounded top corners each bearing seven buttons. Black velvet collar with red top piping bearing a gold-embroidered grenade on each side. The collar closes with three hooks. Cuffs as for the collar. Grenades embroidered on the skirt turnbacks; no buttons on the pocket flaps, two buttons at the rear of the waist and one on each shoulder for the epaulettes. Grey breeches, Hungarian boots with gold trim

Spandau citadel today, showing the round 'Juliusturm'.

and tassel. Normal bicorn. *Surtout:* Dark green and fastened with yellow semi-round buttons, black velvet collar. *Greatcoat:* White, the collar piped in red and bearing two embroidered gold grenades. Cape collar to the waist.

N.C.O.s and Soldiers: The same uniform – busby with red pompon and cords; brass scale epaulettes with red half moons and fringes; red aiguillette, white leatherwork. Trumpeters wear white busbies; white kurtkas faced in black velvet and piped in red (originally this kurtka was red with white facings).

Badges of Rank: As for the Chasseurs à Cheval but with gold aiguillettes. *Armament:* Brass-hilted sabre in a steel sheath with brass fittings; almost straight blade, black belt and slings. Black leather bandolier and pouch with gold ornaments, on the pouch a steel grenade. The bandolier is three inches wide (edged in gold) and has a gilt shield bearing the Polish eagle in silver. Yellow mounted pistols.

Regiments serving with the French Army

The 4th, 7th and 9th Infantry Regiments, serving in Spain in French pay, wore the following uniforms. The 4th Regiment kept its old 1807 uniform with a red collar edged in dark blue, yellow lapels, red cuffs with blue cuff-flaps and the same coloured epaulettes. At the beginning of 1812 the three regiments wore French uniforms, the 4th Regiment also wore the tricolour cockade. The grenadiers had shakos edged in red and their officers also wore shakos. Plumes were red for grenadiers and yellow for the voltigeurs; fusiliers wore pompons in colours according to company as follows: 1st Company – green; 2nd Company – light blue; 3rd Company – yellow; 4th Company – violet. N.C.O.s wore rank stripes, the sergeant-major had lace round his collar. Officers of regimental headquarters and of the fusilier companies wore turnback badges in the form of a crowned 'N'; grenadier officers wore grenades and voltigeurs wore hunting horns. The 7th Regiment had dark blue collars edged crimson, crimson lapels, dark blue cuffs and cuff-flaps with crimson piping; white buttons. The 9th Regiment had red collars edged dark blue, white lapels, red cuffs piped white with dark blue cuff flaps; white buttons.

Somewhat stylized engraving of Prince Poniatowski's death in the River Elster while trying to escape from the scene of France's great defeat at Leipzig.

The Krakus

These light cavalry were a novelty in the Polish Army; instead of trumpeters they had a trooper who carried a pike with a horse's tail attached to the head which was used to give signals. This device was called a 'bunczuk' and its carrier rode a grey horse. There were other innovations in their uniform: the hat consisted of a melon-like crimson 'beret' with a white cockade and plume on the left-hand side and a strip of black sheepskin round the headband; on the top was a white button and white laces came radially from the button down to the headband. Instead of a kurtka they wore a dark blue, single-breasted, full-skirted coat with crimson collar and cuffs and white piping to all edges. The usual cartridge pouch was replaced by the Cossack-style 'tscherkess' which consisted of a set of five metal cartridges on each breast, each with a cap on a silver chain leading to a silver button above the line of cart-ridges. Each group of cartridges was encircled by a white lace (silver for officers) and covered in crimson cloth. The overalls were dark blue with crimson side stripes and black leather inserts. The greatcoat was replaced by a wide grey cape and a hood. Round the waist was a crimson sash; their weapons were pistols, sabres and lances without pennants.

SOURCES

CHELMINSKI, J. VON AND MALIBRAN, A.: *L'Armée du Duche de Varsovie, 1807–15* (Paris, 1913).

GEMBARZEWSKI, BRONISLAW: *Wojsko Polskie* (Warsaw, 1964).

KNÖTEL, HERBERT AND SIEG, HERBERT: *Handbuch der Uniformkunde* (Hamburg, 1966).

LEINHART, DR AND HUMBERT, R.: *Les Uniformes de L'Armée Française*, Vol. V (Paris).

LINDER, KAROL: *Wojsko Polskie Miniatury* (Warsaw, 1967).

The Plates

The basic information on these uniforms is quoted in the preceding section of the text; notes on the individual plates are therefore limited to brief mention of special peculiarities.

A1 Driver, Military Train
The dark or 'slate' blue shown here is typical of Polish uniforms of the eighteenth as well as the nineteenth century. The brass arm-plate bore the number of the column to which the driver was attached, and identified him to military police. All military vehicles in the French – and Polish – armies carried licence plates.

A2 Port-aigle, Grenadier company, 5th Infantry Regiment, 1810–14
The very strong influence of contemporary French designs is obvious; but note that the eagle itself is of Polish design.

A3 Aigle Guard
This sergeant is one of the escort for the preceding figure; the small fanion on the bayonet was used to scare the horses of mounted attackers. The coat is of traditional Polish cut with French grenadier distinctions. French rank badges were worn, but note that Malibran and Chelminski show a deviation – a horizontal gold stripe on the sergeant's cuff in addition to the usual diagonal stripes above it.

B Trumpeter, 14th Kürassiers, parade dress
The trumpeters were the only members of this unit who wore a uniform readily distinguishable from that of the French regiments of this branch.

C Trumpeter, Horse Artillery, full dress
The custom of mounting trumpeters on greys was international at this period, as in later times;

colonels of regiments enjoyed considerable latitude in selecting uniforms for their musicians, hence this gaudy costume. The Polish heavy cavalry usually used English-pattern saddles while lancers and hussars used the Hungarian or 'Bock' saddle. Horse artillery often used light cavalry harness, as here.

D1 Officer, Horse Artillery, full dress
This general colour combination had been traditional Polish and Saxon artillery uniform since the early eighteenth century, but the black fur busby of hussar pattern was a recent innovation.

D2 Voltigeur Cornet, Legion of the Vistula, 1808
Napoleon always tried to keep the Legion firmly under his control, and apart from the rest of the army of the Duchy. This 'dual nationality' is reflected in this uniform of Polish cut, with French shako and voltigeur distinctions. Battle signals were normally given on the *cors du chasse* – cornet or bugle-horn – in the voltigeur companies and light infantry regiments of the French Army, just as the British Rifles used bugles, because the unwieldy drum was considered unsuitable for use by light, fast troops.

D3 Trumpeter, 5th Chasseurs à Cheval, parade dress
Once again, the licence enjoyed by unit commanders has produced a colourful uniform. Note that the single-breasted white coat does not have the usual Polish-cut front worn by dismounted arms. On campaign grey buttoned overalls replaced the breeches, and the expensive white busby was covered with black oil-cloth.

E1 Drum Major, 1st Infantry Regiment
The costume of drum majors of armies of this period would require a separate study of its own, so varied and colourful were the uniforms worn. This figure, after Malibran and Chelminski, shows the tip of the iceberg only! The drum major wears a long-tailed coat of officers' style. As a special distinction his sabre scabbard is brass (or

Entry of the Allied monarchs into Leipzig after the battle of 16–18 October 1813.

gilt?) on gold slings; his crimson *porte-épée* is another mark of his office. The crimson and gold sash was heavily decorated on the chest.

E2 Voltigeur Sergeant, 4th Infantry Regiment, 1810–14
The czapka, the national headgear of Poland, is the most striking feature of this uniform; it is interesting to note that this shape, in much modified and inhibited form, is still to be traced today in Polish military headgear. The front band bears the pierced regimental number. Rank is indicated by the gold top band and silver and crimson cords of the czapka; the silver and crimson epaulette fringes; the gold stripe round the cuff and the conventional diagonal stripes above; and the silver and crimson *porte-épée*. The two gold stripes on the upper left arm are length of service chevrons, again in the French style.

E3 Trooper, 14th Kürassiers, parade dress, 1807–14
Helmet, cuirass, boots, gauntlets and sword are French-made items supplied under a 'lend-lease' arrangement profitable to France! For campaign the impressive boots would give way to short boots worn under grey overalls. For parade the white leather equipment – including the breeches – was pipeclayed. Both men and horses were selected for their size and strength.

F1 Tambour of Fusiliers, 4th Infantry Regiment, field service marching order, 1809
The uniform is conventional. The pack is of brown cowhide with white straps, as in the French Army. Brass drums began to replace the earlier wooden patterns in about 1780, for the sake of lightness and ease of movement. The apron was worn by drummers of all nationalities.

Infantry flag of the kingdom of Poland, 1815: white, corner segments black and red, crimson central circle; gold spearhead, wreaths, ciphers, crowns; silver eagle, cords and tassels. The Russian influence is clear; the new Polish Army uniforms followed the Russian pattern as well.

Eagle of the 2nd Battalion, 13th Infantry Regiment. The white flag has gold fringes, borders and laurel leaves; the central motif is an oil-painting in blue and white.

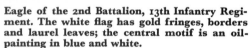

Sabretache of an officer of Polish hussars.

Battle of Hanau, 31 October 1813. Here Napoleon's army, fleeing after the disaster at Leipzig, pushed through an Austro-Bavarian force to cross the Rhine and reach the refuge of France.

F2 Sous-lieutenant, 13th Hussars, full dress, 1806–14
The two Polish hussar regiments, the 10th and 13th, were the most decorative units in the army – this branch has had an image of unequalled glamour, in all national armies, since the late years of the eighteenth century. The colours reflect the national colours of Poland. The silver lacing on the thighs increased in size and number of lines according to rank.

F3 Grenadier, 13th Infantry Regiment, 1809–14
The white uniform was unique in the army of the duchy; this regiment was raised in 1809 from Austrian prisoners from Galician areas – i.e. regions which had belonged to the kingdom of Poland before its partition between Russia, Prussia and Austria. It is likely that the white Austrian

single-breasted jackets were modified by simply sewing on false half-lapels, and cuff-flaps could have been added in the same manner.

G1 Gunner, Horse Artillery, stable dress
The fine uniforms worn on parade in Napoleonic days were recognized, even then, as being a shade impractical for such tasks as 'mucking out' the squadron stables, and a much simpler everyday costume was devised for these tasks. The sleeves of the working-dress coats worn by some armies were only laced in position, and could be removed in summer.

G2 Trooper, Lancers, stable dress
The *zipfelmütze* or forage cap was usually made up from old uniforms by the unit tailors, and the

design often varied according to the colonel's taste. The overalls would also be the normal campaign dress, although breeches and high boots often accompanied the regiments in the baggage train; Napoleon had strict ideas about the occasions on which his troops could properly dispense with full uniform, and where circumstances allowed would order full dress on the battlefield.

G3 Trooper, Kürassiers, stable dress

Due to the complexity of the code of facing colours within this branch, it is not possible to identify the regiment with which this man served from the scant distinctions visible on the working uniform.

H1 Brigadier-Trompette, Chevau-légers Polonais de la Garde, marching order, 1810–14

This corporal trumpeter wears the oil-cloth czapka cover, buttoned overalls, and buttoned-across crimson kurtka of marching order. Little need be said about this famous regiment, always the apple of Napoleon's eye; many of the men followed their Emperor to Elba in 1814. Their lesser-known sister unit, the 3rd (Lithuanian) Lancers of the Guard, wore the same basic uniform, but with gold lace and metal replacing the silver, during their short career.

H2 Officer, Krakus, 1812

Raised in Lithuania during the 1812 campaign, this unit was clothed in a uniform which displayed strong cossack influence. The colours employed once again reflect Polish national colours.

H3 Trooper, Lithuanian Tartars of the Guard, 1812

The uniform of this regiment has long been the subject of controversy; since the very limited number of original sources are at variance, it will probably remain so. The fact that this unit of almost Asiatic dress was raised in Poland in 1812 is a reminder that in centuries gone by Poland was a much stronger nation, with territories so widespread that she rivalled even Russia. Officers of this unit wore jackets with much more elaborate embroidery.